Invitations to Personal Reading
Curriculum Foundation Classroom Library
Scott, Foresman and Company

Adventures in Many Lands

Henry Reed's Journey	Keith Robertson
The *Minnow* Leads to Treasure	A. Philippa Pearce
The Singing Cave	Eilís Dillon
"What Then, Raman?"	Shirley Arora

Science and Nature

The Giant Golden Book of Biology	Gerald Ames and Rose Wyler
Jets and Rockets and How They Work	William P. Gottlieb
The Peaceful Atom	Bernice Kohn
Sea Pup Again	Archie Binns
Stormy	James Kjelgaard

Biography and Historical Fiction

Across Five Aprils	Irene Hunt
America's Ethan Allen	Stewart Holbrook
From the Eagle's Wing	Hildegarde Swift
Trace Through the Forest	Barbara Robinson
Tree in the Trail	Holling C. Holling

Legends, Myths, and Other Tales

The Golden Treasury of Myths and Legends	adapted by Anne T. White
Ride with the Sun	edited by Harold Courlander

Science Fiction and Fantasy

Bob Fulton's Amazing Soda-Pop Stretcher	Jerome Beatty, Jr.
The City Under the Back Steps	Evelyn S. Lampman
Danny Dunn, Time Traveler	Jay Williams and Raymond Abrashkin

Books Too Good to Miss

Mr. Twigg's Mistake	Robert Lawson
North to Freedom	Anne Holm
The Story of Design	Marion Downer
The Twenty-One Balloons	William Pène du Bois

Poetry

The Charge of the Light Brigade	Alfred Lord Tennyson
The Moment of Wonder	edited by Richard Lewis

THE PEACEFUL ATOM

THE PEACEFUL ATOM

by
BERNICE KOHN

illustrated by
ZENOWIJ ONYSHKEWYCH

PRENTICE-HALL, INC.
ENGLEWOOD CLIFFS, NEW JERSEY

Special Scott, Foresman and Company Edition
for the *Invitations to Personal Reading* Program

OTHER PRENTICE-HALL BOOKS BY THE SAME AUTHOR:

Our Tiny Servants: Molds and Yeasts
illustrated by John Kaufmann

Computers at Your Service
illustrated by Aliki

The Peaceful Atom, by Bernice Kohn

Library of Congress Catalog Card Number: 63-9054

Printed in the United States of America

This edition is printed and distributed by
Scott, Foresman and Company
by special arrangement with Prentice-Hall, Inc.

CONTENTS

THE ATOMIC AGE

Do you ever look at the things around you and wonder what they are made of? You may see a table that is made of wood. But what is *wood* made of? What are *you* made of? What are carrots made of, and birds, and bikes, and baseballs?

Every single thing in the world is made of *atoms*. Atoms are so tiny that there are only a few microscopes in the whole world powerful enough to show them. It would take about 20 million atoms to make a dot as big as this one over the letter *i*. In fact, if you had one atom for every single person in the states of Pennsylvania and California, you could fit them all on the head of a pin!

But, small as they are, atoms are the building blocks that make everything. You certainly don't look anything like an elephant—do you? But you are both made of atoms! You don't look anything like a scrambled egg, either—or a washcloth, or a refrigerator—but they are all made of atoms, too!

Atoms are everywhere, they are everything—and you should learn something about them because you live in the atomic age.

Why is this the atomic age? Were atoms just discovered? No, they weren't. People have known about atoms for a long time.

Then what is different about this age? The difference is that we have learned how to make atoms work for us. We call this work *atomic energy*.

When your father and mother were children, no one had ever heard of atomic energy. Energy for heat, light, and to operate machinery came from a few main sources.

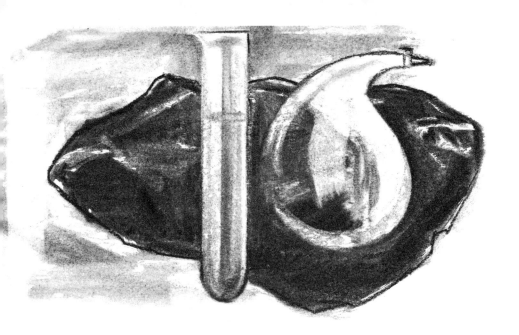

Some came from water power, a little from wind power —but almost all energy came from burning fuels.

The chief fuels of the world for many years have been coal, oil, and natural gas. These are all *fossil fuels*. That means that they were made millions of years ago and have lain trapped in the earth ever since. Once these fuels are used up, there will be no way to replace them. There just won't be any more.

By the early years of the 1900's, some people were beginning to worry about fuel. There wasn't any shortage yet, and there wouldn't be for a long time. There were still new coal mines and new oil wells being discovered. But some day, the last one *would* be discovered, the fuels would be all used—and then what?

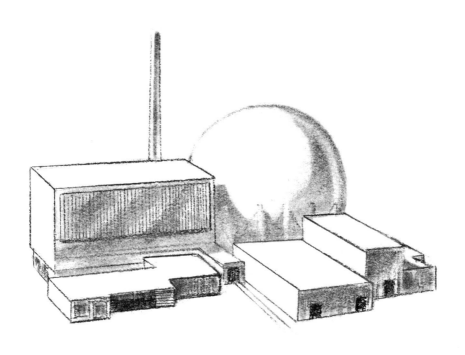

atomic power plant

As new industries developed all over the world, the need for power grew—and so did the worry. And then suddenly, in 1942, one of the greatest discoveries of all time was made. The atomic age was born and the perfect fuel was found.

Atomic energy can do things never before dreamed of. Atoms, without any fire, without any noise, can run a huge electricity plant. The atoms in one pound of fuel can keep the lights burning in your home for 1000 years!

Atoms can send a large ship back and forth across the ocean many times—on one small load of fuel!

Atoms can keep hamburger fresh for weeks without freezing!

Atoms can sometimes cure sick people!

Atoms can find leaks in pipes, and can test the rubber in a set of car tires!

Atoms, in many ways, can make life easier, healthier, and better for us.

What are these wonderful atoms, anyway? Let's find out.

Democritus

✳2

THE SMALLEST THING THERE IS

The story of atoms begins about two thousand years ago, in ancient Greece. There, a wise man named Democritus started to think about what things were made of. Democritus reasoned that you could take a little piece of anything at all—wood, metal, even candy—and cut it in half. Then you could cut the halves in half. Then you could cut *those* pieces in half. And so on. But finally, Democritus said, you would get to particles so tiny that they could not be divided any more. He called these smallest particles *atoms,* from the Greek word *atomos* which means *indivisible.*

It was hard for people to believe that everything in the world was made of atoms. They soon forgot about Democritus and his strange ideas. Atoms were forgotten for almost two thousand years.

But during the eighteenth century, European scientists again became interested in the structure of things and began to experiment. There were some curious discoveries.

Chemists found that a substance like water could be separated into two other substances, *hydrogen* and *oxygen*. But hydrogen and oxygen couldn't be broken down into any other chemicals no matter what the chemists did. They could easily change table salt into *sodium* and *chlorine*. But no matter how hard they tried, they weren't able to break down sodium and chlorine into anything else.

14

So scientists decided that most of the things around us—water, salt, wood, animals—were made of combinations of substances. They called the combinations *chemical compounds*. They called the substances that couldn't be broken down *elements*.

We now know of more than one hundred elements. In the year 1800, about half that number had been discovered. And it was at about this time that an Englishman, John Dalton, came along with the first really scientific *atomic theory*.

Dalton said that all elements are made of atoms, and the atoms of any particular element are always the same. An atom of carbon is always like every other atom of carbon. And, Dalton went on, atoms of different elements have different weights. An atom of carbon weighs more than an atom of hydrogen. An atom of oxygen weighs more than an atom of carbon.

Dalton noticed that atoms combined in different ways according to their weights. Water is made of hydrogen and oxygen. But it takes *two* hydrogen atoms with *one* oxygen atom to make water. This smallest unit of water is called a *molecule*. A molecule is the smallest possible amount of any chemical compound.

Another contribution that Dalton made was the use of shorthand symbols to stand for chemical elements.

John Dalton

Today, we use a system which grew out of Dalton's. Instead of calling the water molecule "two atoms of hydrogen and one atom of oxygen," we call hydrogen "H" and oxygen "O" and write, simply, H_2O. The symbol for carbon is "C" and carbon dioxide may be written CO_2. This means that one carbon atom and two oxygen atoms combine to form one molecule of carbon dioxide.

John Dalton was a great scientist and almost everything in his atomic theory turned out to be correct. Only one of his ideas we now know to be wrong. And that idea went all the way back to Democritus. They both thought that the atom was the smallest possible particle, and that it could never be divided.

It certainly seemed to be so. But astonishing things about atoms began to turn up around the end of the 1800's. No one knew it yet, but men were going to change atoms—and atoms were going to change the world!

✳ 3

THE MYSTERY OF THE RAYS

In 1895, a German scientist, Wilhelm K. Roentgen (RENT-gen), was experimenting with a special kind of electrical tube. He had covered one end of the tube with black paper. Nearby was a screen that glowed when light shone on it.

Roentgen happened to glance at the screen—and could hardly believe his eyes. It was glowing—but there was no light coming from the covered tube! This seemed impossible—but there it was.

Later, when someone asked Roentgen what he thought, he made a true scientist's reply.

He said, "I did not think. I investigated!"

Roentgen didn't know what the rays were, so he decided to call them *X rays*. He found that they could pass not only through black paper, but through many other substances as well. They went easily through cloth or wood, but were stopped by metal. Roentgen found that the mysterious rays could shine right through the soft parts of the body, but they were stopped by bones.

18

Wilhelm K. Roentgen

X ray of a broken leg bone

Here was a useful discovery, indeed. Just imagine how valuable it was to a doctor to be able to take a shadow picture of a broken bone so that he could see how to set it. Your dentist probably uses Roentgen's X rays to take pictures of your teeth to look for cavities.

Roentgen's discovery stirred up a great deal of interest. Perhaps there were other kinds of rays. Scientists began to search for them.

One of the searchers was Antoine Henri Becquerel (Beck-er-EL), a Frenchman. In 1896, Becquerel was experimenting with some crystals of a uranium salt. These crystals gave off a glow after being exposed to sunlight.

One day, Becquerel was all ready to test the glow on a photographic film. But just as he was about to start, the sky turned cloudy. The experiment couldn't be done without sunlight, so Becquerel wrapped his film in a piece of black paper, put the crystal on top, and put the package away in a drawer.

uranium

Antoine Henri Becquerel

The sun stayed hidden for several days and Becquerel couldn't continue with his experiment. But he decided to develop his film anyway. He was astonished to find a black spot right in the middle, just where the uranium crystal had been! That meant that even without any sunlight, the crystal had given off rays of its own! Another mystery!

Becquerel tested several compounds that contained uranium and found that they all gave off similar rays. Why?

Marie Curie

One of the scientists who heard about Becquerel's work was a young Polish woman working in Paris. Her name was *Marie Curie* (Cu-REE).

Madame Curie wondered if uranium were the only element to give off rays. With the help of her husband, Pierre, she began to test every known element for rays. She decided to call this ability to give off rays *radioactivity*.

After many tests, Madame Curie found that the element *thorium* was also radioactive. So, the Curies reasoned, if there were *two* radioactive elements, there were probably more. And they continued to search.

Then one day, a strange thing happened. The Curies were busy refining uranium from its ore, *pitchblende*. But they suddenly noticed that the ore seemed to be more radioactive than the uranium itself! How could this be? The only explanation, Madame Curie thought, was that there must be another, stronger, radioactive element in pitchblende.

In 1898, after working through tons of pitchblende, the Curies succeeded in separating a speck of a new element that was 900 times more radioactive than uranium! They named the new element *radium*.

The Curies and other scientists were very excited. Here were three elements—uranium, thorium, and radium—all giving off powerful rays. Where did the rays come from? Scientists were sure they could only come from the atoms of the elements themselves. But how could that be? There couldn't be anything smaller than an atom. Or could there? The scientists didn't know. It was a real mystery.

✳4

WHAT'S IN AN ATOM?

Every mystery is sure to attract some people who wish to solve it. And the mystery of radioactivity was no exception. Scientists in many parts of the world began to search for clues. Little by little, they found them. It wasn't until the 1930's that the last pieces of the puzzle began to fall into place—the structure of the atom was finally clear.

But before we talk about the structure of atoms, let's talk about the structure of houses. Many houses are built of wood, shingles, and glass. However, even though the houses are built of the same materials, they may not look anything alike. Some are ranch houses, some are split levels, and some are colonial houses.

On the other hand, sometimes a builder puts up a large development in which all the houses are exactly the same. If a new friend tells you that he lives in the Shady Acres development, you can picture his house. It is just like every other house in Shady Acres.

Are you wondering what this has to do with atoms? Well, all atoms are built of the same principal materials.

They are called *protons, electrons,* and *neutrons.* And just as a ranch house never looks exactly like a colonial house, an atom of one element never looks exactly like the atom of another element.

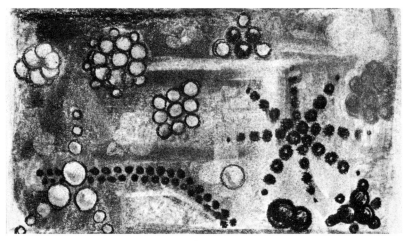

atoms

But like the Shady Acres houses, every atom of the *same* element looks exactly like every other. A hydrogen atom looks like every other hydrogen atom. A carbon atom looks like every other carbon atom. But a hydrogen atom *never* looks like a carbon atom.

Atoms are like houses in still another way, too. Even though the building materials used in two houses or two atoms are the same, the finished structure of a house or an atom depends on the way the materials are arranged.

26

If an atom could be made large enough for you to see, you might think you were watching a satellite (or a fleet of satellites) going around and around one or more planets.

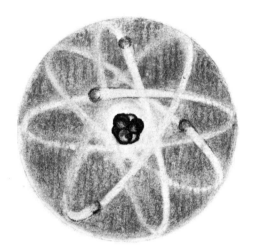

an atom

The planet—or center of the atom—is called the *nucleus*. It is made mostly of protons and neutrons. The little satellites circling around the nucleus are always electrons.

Ordinary atoms always have the same number of protons as they do of electrons. This number is called the *atomic number*. No two elements have the same atomic number. It is the number of protons and electrons that tells us what kind of atom it is. When there are two protons in the nucleus and two electrons circling around it, we know that we have an atom of *helium*. If it doesn't have two protons and two electrons, it isn't helium.

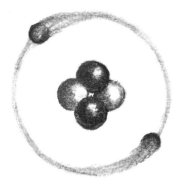

helium atom

A helium atom also has two neutrons in its nucleus. Usually, no atom can change its number of protons or electrons and remain the same kind of atom—but it *can* change its number of neutrons.

Atoms of the same element, but with different numbers of neutrons in the nucleus, are called *isotopes*. Some elements have only one isotope, some have as many as eight or ten.

an isotope of helium

Uranium has three main isotopes. The most common kind of uranium has 92 protons, 146 neutrons, and—of course—92 electrons. (Did you remember that the number of electrons has to match the number of protons?)

Adding up the total particles in the nucleus, we see that $92 + 146 = 238$, so this kind of uranium is called uranium-238. There is an isotope that has 143 neutrons, so this is uranium-235 because $92 + 143 = 235$. The last isotope has 142 neutrons and is uranium-234.

The heaviest part of any atom is the nucleus. Protons and neutrons are very much heavier than electrons. And then there is lots and lots of empty space. If the nucleus of the hydrogen atom (which has only one proton) were enlarged to the size of a tennis ball, the electron would be a half mile away!

A whole atom is so tiny that it is almost impossible to imagine anything so small. It would take 250 million of some kinds of atoms to measure one inch. But it would take *fifty thousand* times as many electrons to cover the same inch!

⁕ 5

A SEARCH BEGINS

Now we know a lot about the structure of the atom—but we still haven't solved the mystery of the rays. So let's do that right now.

A radioactive atom is really a temporary atom. It is unbalanced and shoots off parts of itself in order to become balanced. As the atom gives up protons, neutrons, and electrons, we say that it *decays*. If your tooth decays, a small part of it crumbles away. And the same thing happens to an atom.

We know that if an atom changes its number of protons it becomes a different kind of atom. And that is just what happens to radioactive elements. Uranium, thorium, and radium all change into lead. Other radioactive elements decay to different elements.

When an atom decays, it gives off three different kinds of particles. These are named for the first three letters of the Greek alphabet and are called *alpha* particles, *beta* particles, and *gamma* rays.

radioactive decay

Some radioactive elements decay very quickly—in a few seconds—but some take millions of years. As the element decays, its atoms shoot off particles. The larger the amount of the element, the more particles it shoots off. But as the element decays, there is less and less of it left. If at first it gives up 100 particles a second, it will, as its size decreases, give up only 90 particles a second. Then it will give up only 80 particles a second, and so on.

This slowing down makes it very hard to measure how long it will take the element to completely decay. It is much easier to figure out when it will be *half* decayed. And so we never speak of the life of a radio-active element. We speak of its *half-life*.

When the radioactive element that started giving up 100 particles a second gets down to losing only 50 particles a second, we know that half of its radioactivity has been used up. Radium has a half-life of 1,690 years. Uranium has a half-life of 4,500 million years!

Radioactivity is very interesting, but before we can understand its real importance, we must learn a little about energy.

To most of us, energy means "pep." To a scientist, energy means *the ability to do work*. Energy is not a "thing." You can't see it. You can only see—or hear—or feel—what it does. Energy never disappears, but it can be changed from one form to another.

When you swing a bat and wallop a ball, part of the energy you use makes the ball whiz through the air. If you use energy to clap your hands, part of the energy is

changed to sound, and you hear a noise. If electrical energy is used in a light bulb, part of the energy is changed into light and part into heat.

When we burn wood for heat, we are using energy that the tree took from the sun. When we burn coal or oil, we are using the energy of sunlight that was stored many millions of years ago.

All of this energy is stored in the atoms of the wood, coal, or oil. But when we burn these materials for fuel, we release only the energy of the *electrons*.

Now do you remember, back in the last chapter, we said that the nucleus is the heavy part of the atom? And that the electrons are very light? Well, the nucleus is so very, very heavy for its tiny size, that it cannot be compared to anything else in the world. If a nucleus were as large as a grain of rice, it would weigh two million tons! Nothing so small could weigh so much unless it were extremely tightly packed together. It takes a great deal of energy to pack anything that solidly.

By the middle of the 1930's, scientists were beginning to think about the huge amount of energy that would be released if the nucleus could be split. The scientific name for splitting is *fission*.

Just suppose, the scientists thought, you could split a nucleus and its neutrons would come flying out—and each neutron would strike like a bullet at another nucleus and make *that* one split? And all the new flying neutrons would split other atoms? This would be a *chain reaction.*

If man could produce a chain reaction, there would be such energy as the world never dreamed of! In many different countries, men thought, and dreamed, and worked—the search for the nuclear chain reaction was on!

✳6

JOURNEY
TO THE NEW WORLD

It was a gray winter morning. The date was December 2, 1942. The place, The University of Chicago. Here at Stagg Field, under the football stands, was a large empty room that had once been a squash court.

None of the students who hurried by on the way to class paid much attention to a few men who passed through the door into the long unused room. No one knew that in that room one of the greatest events in the history of science was about to take place. No one knew that the atomic age would be born that day.

The men who had gathered in the secret room were some of the finest scientists in the world. The leader of the group was Enrico Fermi (En-REE-ko FER-mee), an Italian scientist who had come to the United States.

For some weeks the men had been quietly at work, carefully stacking a huge pile of pure graphite bricks. Here and there among the bricks they placed pieces of uranium. Fermi believed that when the pile reached a certain size, a chain reaction would start. By December 2, the size seemed to be right.

Enrico Fermi

Inside the pile were three control rods. They were made of cadmium, an element which soaks up flying neutrons like a sponge. With the rods in place, no reaction could take place. When the rods were withdrawn, the reaction would begin.

To make sure that the pile would not get out of hand, the three control rods were operated in three different ways. The first one was controlled by an electrical switch and was completely automatic. The second, called ZIP, was tied to a rope in the balcony. In case of emergency, there was a man ready with an axe. He had only to chop the rope and ZIP would go crashing back into the pile. The third rod was moved by hand.

It was time to begin. Fermi gave the signal for the automatic rod to be withdrawn. Immediately, the counters which measured radioactivity began to tick.

Then Fermi gave the command, "ZIP out!" ZIP was drawn up on its balcony rope and the ticking of the counters at once became faster.

Then Fermi turned to the man who controlled the last rod. This rod was marked in feet and inches, and Fermi said: "Pull it out to thirteen feet."

All eyes were on the instruments. Not yet. A little more. Pull it out another foot. Not yet. The men grew more and more tense as the careful work went on.

chain reaction

Finally, at about 3:25 in the afternoon, Fermi made a last check of his instruments and his calculations. Then he said: "Pull it out another foot. This is going to do it!"

No one dared breathe. The ticks of the counters became so rapid they sounded like a steady hum. The pointers on the instruments swung all the way over—and stayed there. The first atomic chain reaction had been achieved!

The pile was allowed to run for 28 minutes. Then the control rods were put back. Suddenly, all was quiet. There were no ticks from the counters.

Not only had these men started a chain reaction, they had also been able to stop it. At last man could control the energy of the atom.

One of the men present, Arthur H. Compton, ran to the phone to call James B. Conant, chairman of the U. S. National Defense Research Committee. But since our country was at war in 1942, it wasn't safe to talk about this important secret over the telephone. And so, on the spur of the moment, a quick-witted and historic conversation took place.

Compton said: "Jim, you'll be interested to know that the Italian navigator has just landed in the new world."

Conant, who knew of the experiments that had been going on, understood at once. He said: "Is that so? Were the natives friendly?"

And Compton replied: "Everyone landed safe and happy."

This was the first day of the atomic age. The reactor had been started, had been stopped—and had produced enough power to light one small flashlight bulb!

TINY ATOMS, BIG POWER

Atomic power has grown quickly since that day in 1942. Atomic power plants now make electricity to light large cities in many parts of the world.

Atomic power doesn't make electricity directly. It makes heat. The heat turns into steam. Then the steam turns turbines and the spinning turbines drive the generators which make electric current.

Pressurized Water Reactor

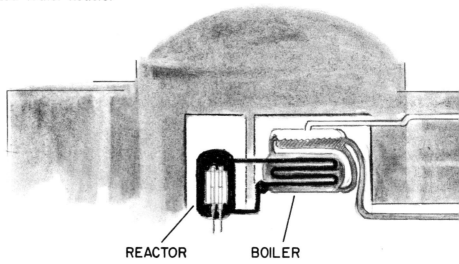

REACTOR   BOILER

Ordinary steam power plants depend on fossil fuels—coal, oil, or gas—to make heat. It has been figured out that if only coal were used for fuel, the world's supply would be used up in 350 years. Oil and gas would last for 40 years. But there are enough nuclear fuels to last for at least 8,500 years!

There are several kinds of atomic power plants, but the best known is the Pressurized Water Reactor. This long name is usually abbreviated to PWR.

The PWR isn't really very different from Fermi's pile in Chicago. There is the same big stack of atomic fuel—usually uranium—with control rods sticking out of holes in the fuel bars. Just like Fermi's pile, when the control rods are pushed in they soak up the flying neutrons and

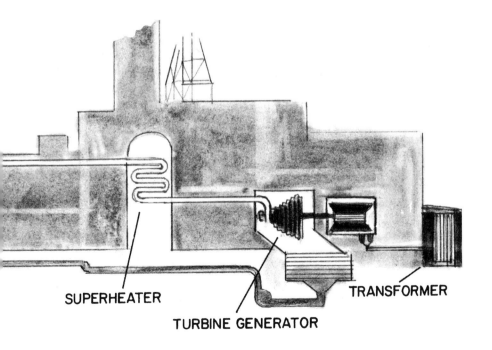

SUPERHEATER

TURBINE GENERATOR

TRANSFORMER

there is no reaction. When the control rods are pulled out, the chain reaction takes place.

One of the curious things about a chain reaction is that it won't work if the neutrons are flying too fast. They hit the new atoms at such great speed that they just bounce off and keep going. In order for the neutrons to do their splitting job, they have to be slowed down. Fermi used graphite bricks for this purpose. The PWR uses water, which works very well. And the water also serves another purpose. It absorbs the great heat which is formed in the reactor.

Now, everyone knows that when water is heated to a high temperature, it boils. But *this* water must not boil. To prevent its boiling, the water is kept under very high pressure, and that is how the Pressurized Water Reactor got its name.

The water is sealed in special tubes and reaches a temperature of about 600° F. The tubes then heat *other* water which turns into steam.

A simpler kind of atomic power plant is the Boiling Water Reactor, or BWR. The BWR is just a tank which holds a reactor and water. In this case, the water is *not* under pressure and the heat released by the chain reaction makes it boil. The steam which comes from the boiling water goes directly to the turbine.

Whether they use PWRs or BWRs, atomic power plants don't look very much like ordinary plants. There is no smoke, no dirt, and no fire. Everything is controlled by automatic switches and there may be no more than two or three men in sight.

The first atomic power plant in the world was built in the U.S.S.R. and went into service in 1954. There are now a number of such plants in the United States. Two of the largest are the Duquesne Light Company at Shippingport, Pennsylvania, near Pittsburgh, and Consolidated Edison's Indian Point Plant, in New York State.

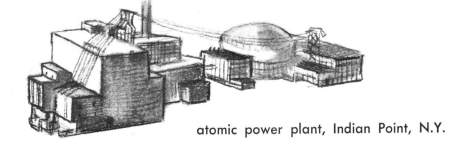

atomic power plant, Indian Point, N.Y.

Important as atomic power is to cities, it is of even greater importance to faraway places where fuel is hard to get. For example, at the U.S. Army's Camp Century in Greenland, far above the Arctic Circle, obtaining power had always been a problem. The cost of shipping coal or oil to such a place was so high that it was impractical. People had to get along with very little heat or power. But not any more.

Camp Century's new atomic power plant supplies heat and electricity for all. In a whole year the plant uses only 40 pounds of atomic fuel. If it ran on diesel fuel, it would need 850,000 gallons a year!

One of the strangest things about some atomic reactors (called *breeder reactors*), is that they make new fuel as they go along. If the fuel is uranium, it is usually a mixture of uranium-235 and uranium-238. Only the U-235 can be used for the chain reaction. But when the flying neutrons from the U-235 strike the U-238, it turns into a new element, *plutonium.* Plutonium is a fine atomic fuel, just like U-235. In some atomic furnaces there is more fuel at the end of the reaction than the furnace had to start with!

Just look at all the advantages of the atomic power plant: It solves the problem of the disappearing fossil fuels. The plant is almost completely automatic and can be run by just a few men. It saves the cost of shipping heavy fuels to distant places. Some atomic plants make new fuel as they run. Also, the ashes of an atomic furnace are highly valuable for a number of purposes, as you will soon see.

With so many advantages, there is no question that the coal or oil power plant will soon be a thing of the past. It may be that during your lifetime, most of the world's power will come from atomic reactors.

✳ 8

ATOMS FOR TRANSPORT

In the year 1819, the world was agog because a steamship had crossed the Atlantic Ocean. How wonderful it seemed! The ship was called the *Savannah*. She carried wood and coal for her steam boilers, but the ship wasn't large enough to carry fuel for the 30-day trip. There was steam for the first seven days, and then the *Savannah* continued under sails.

Today, there is a new *Savannah* which can travel for three and one half years on one load of fuel! She is called the Nuclear Ship *Savannah* and her fuel is uranium. Instead of a steam boiler she has a Pressurized Water Reactor.

The *Savannah* is a beautiful white ship nearly 600 feet long. But when you look at her, there seems to be something missing. There aren't any smokestacks! Of course there aren't any smokestacks, because there isn't any smoke!

The N.S. *Savannah* has a speed of 21 knots. She can carry 9,400 tons of cargo, 60 passengers, and a crew of 110. On only 700 pounds of fuel, she can take this heavy load around the world 12 times!

N.S. *Savannah*

Atomic reactors are already in use on ships and submarines and they may soon be used for other types of transportation. Experiments have been made on atomic tractors which would pull long trains of sleds in the Arctic. And there has been some interest among railroad people in atomic locomotives.

The most serious experiments, so far, with atomic locomotives, have been made in the U.S.S.R. That country, because of its vast size, has an unusual amount of freight traffic. Trains now use up one quarter of all the coal and oil produced there. The Russians have completed the design for an atomic locomotive that will have a speed of 75 miles an hour while pulling a load of 4,000 tons. It will travel for almost a year without new fuel, and will go from Moscow to Riga and back (about 1,000 miles) on a piece of uranium the size of a marble!

Designers here and abroad have also started to think about atomic airplanes. One type of design would use a reactor similar to the power plant reactor. It would make steam, the steam would drive a turbine, and the turbine would turn the propellers.

Another design would work on the turbojet principle and wouldn't need steam. Air would be scooped in and heated by the reactor, then shot out of the rear jets, driving the plane ahead.

atomic plane

However, there are serious problems in designing an atomic plane. One of the hardest to solve is the radioactive exhaust that would come from the reactor. All of the waste products of an atomic furnace are highly radioactive and very dangerous to humans. They can cause serious injury or death. People have to be protected from radioactive materials by heavy shielding of concrete or lead. On a plane, of course, the weight of such a heavy shield would create a difficult problem. The shield would weigh more than the gasoline the atomic fuel replaced.

In time, however, there will probably be a solution to the problem, and atomic planes will be made. There will be no worry about running out of fuel. Such things as head winds, long flights across water, and fuel leaks will no longer be threats to the safety of plane passengers. And when the shielding. problem is solved, instead of carrying 50 tons of gasoline, a big plane will be able to carry 50 tons more of people or cargo.

All of these possibilities are just ideas now. But someday, perhaps, you will chuckle over the old-fashioned days before A-trains and A-planes—or, even A-cars!

51

ATOMS THAT TRACE

Do you remember what isotopes are? They are atoms of the same element, which have different numbers of neutrons in their *nuclei* (NEWK-lee-eye), the plural of nucleus. Some isotopes, when struck by flying neutrons in a reactor, begin to give off rays, like radium. These isotopes are called *radioisotopes*.

Some radioisotopes are made on purpose by putting certain elements into a reactor. But many radioisotopes are made in all atomic reactors as a natural product of the chain reaction. After the fuel has been used, the radioisotopes are removed from the ashes.

Most elements have at least one radioisotope and many have several. They have thousands of important uses and new ones are found every day.

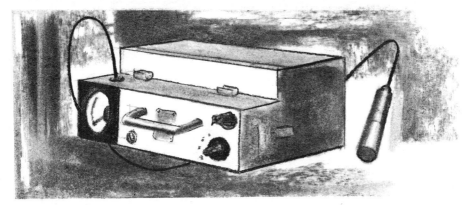

Geiger counter

There are a few properties of radioisotopes which make them useful. One of them is the fact that they give off radiation and so they can always be found with a Geiger (GUY-ger) counter. This is an instrument which ticks when it is struck by an atomic ray. With the help of a counter, radioisotopes can be used as tracers, or tags.

Tracers are used in dozens of interesting ways. One is to find leaks in pipes. Sometimes there is a leaky pipe buried in the floors or walls of a building. How can you find out where the leak is without tearing the building apart? It is very simple. Just add a tiny bit of a radio-isotope to the water in the pipe. Then move a Geiger counter along the floor or wall in which the pipe is enclosed. When the ticks stop—or continue, but spread out over a large area—you have found the leak.

A similar trick is often used in the oil industry. Sometimes the same pipeline is used for oil and for gasoline.

A worker at the far end of the pipeline has the job of turning off a valve when the oil stops coming through, and turning on a different valve to send the gasoline to the proper tank. But how does he know when the oil is finished and the gasoline is about to start? There's nothing to it. A dash of radioisotope is mixed with the last gallon of oil. The worker keeps his Geiger counter on the pipe. When it begins to tick, it's time to make the change.

If you had a tire factory, how would you find out which kind of rubber gave the best wear? You could

using a tracer

make four different kinds of tires and add a bit of radioisotope to the rubber of each. With the tires on a car, instead of driving thousands of miles, as in the past, you
could drive just a short distance. As the tires turned, tiny
bits of rubber would wear off. A Geiger counter moved
over the tire tracks would tell you right away which tire
lost the least rubber. Tire companies use this test widely.

Radioisotopes mixed with wax or polish tell how much
is left on a car after washing. Radioactive dirt smeared
on cloth tells which detergent does the best washing job.
If radioisotopes are mixed with the liquid in a tank, a

Geiger counter on the outside of the tank can tell where the top of the liquid is. This is much easier than sending a man all the way to the top of the tank to measure the contents with a dip stick.

Scientists have made great use of the radioisotope carbon-14. Carbon-14 occurs naturally in the air and is taken in by all living plants. It is also taken in by all people or animals who eat plants. Once a living thing dies, however, it does not take in any more carbon-14. Now it happens that carbon-14 has a very long half-life —about 5,000 years. So even if a plant or an animal has been dead for 25,000 years, there are still slight traces of carbon-14 left. By measuring the quantity with a counter and comparing it to the quantity in a living plant or animal of the same kind, scientists can tell the age of very old things.

When ancient writings about Biblical times, called the Dead Sea Scrolls, were found, they were wrapped in linen. The linen, made from the fibers of the flax plant, was tested for carbon-14. It was found to be about 2,000 years old. The same method has been used to find the age of ancient wood, leather, cloth, bones—and even mummies!

Radioisotope tracers have been of great benefit to farmers. Mixed with fertilizers, they can be followed with a Geiger counter to see just how the plant uses the fertilizer and how fast. Tracers have shown how certain feeds make animals grow fatter. They help in the study of milk production by cows, egg production by chickens, and growth of wool on sheep.

Perhaps the most important of all tracer uses is in medicine. Radioactive iodine, or iodine-131, is used to find diseases of the thyroid gland. The patient swallows a small dose of the tracer and a counter shows how fast it is taken in by the thyroid gland. This shows how active the gland is. Tracers also help to find brain tumors. And they can be used to follow the circulation of the blood. If an artery is blocked, a person may die because his blood can't circulate. A counter can find the trouble spot and help save a life.

Radioisotopes which are used as medical tracers are not harmful to the body. They are carefully selected to have a very short half-life. Their radioactivity is gone before it can do damage. Also, they are used in tiny quantities.

While radioisotopes do wonderful jobs as tracers, they can do some other very interesting things, too. Let's see what some of them are.

✳10

ATOMS TO CHANGE ATOMS

When the rays of a radioactive substance strike the atoms of another substance, they may cause changes. We call the exposure to rays *irradiation* (ir-rade-ee-AY-shun). One of the changes caused by irradiation is called ionization (eye-on-i-ZAY-shun).

Radioisotopes do many important jobs for us by irradiation. In industry, certain petroleum and other materials are changed by irradiation into special fuels, oils, and even synthetic rubber.

Irradiation is used to improve the quality of plastics and to vulcanize rubber. It used to take several hours to vulcanize with heat. A few minutes of irradiation does the same job.

The food industry has begun to experiment with irradiation as a new way to sterilize food. Items which normally spoil quickly, such as hamburger, sausage, cheese, and bread, are exposed to radiation. The rays destroy all of the bacteria that cause food to spoil. The food is immediately sealed in airtight plastic bags. It will remain

irradiation prevents sprouting

perfectly fresh for months—or even years. This process may make the canning or freezing of food completely unnecessary.

Even foods which generally keep well, such as onions or potatoes, can be helped by irradiation. The treatment kills any insects that might be in the sack, and also keeps the vegetables from sprouting. A treated potato will keep for a very long time. A number of experiments have been done with potatoes. Before long you will probably see irradiated potatoes for sale in your market.

Irradiation can even improve food crops and other plants while they are still being grown. Changes caused by the rays have already created new and better varieties of corn, peanuts, and oats. The same dose of irradiation works in another way, too—it kills the insects which damage the crops.

Irradiation used in certain medicines can destroy a patient's diseased tissue. Many forms of cancer are treated by this method. In some cases, the patient is in-

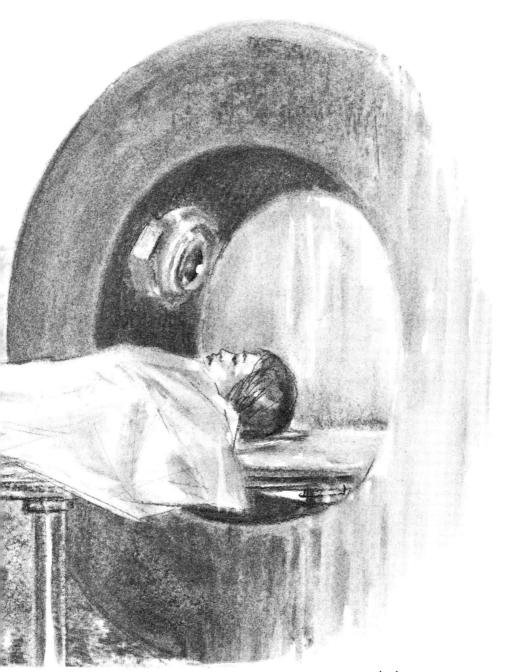

cobalt treatment

jected with a radioisotope. In other cases, he is just exposed to its rays, which are projected from a special machine. Sometimes, tiny bits of isotope, called *seeds*, are actually placed directly in the cancer. Other patients are asked to drink the isotope in a special preparation called a "radioactive cocktail."

Besides their many uses as tracers and irradiators, isotopes have great value as substitutes for expensive X-ray machines. The rays can pass through many materials and, by making a picture on a film underneath, can show differences in thickness or other flaws. Some of the materials that are inspected this way are sheet metal, paper, rubber, and plastics. Also, piston rings for auto engines, and airplane engine valves.

Doctors, too, can use radioisotopes instead of X rays. An X-ray machine is a huge piece of equipment which needs a special room and costs thousands of dollars. A radioisotope machine is about the size of a large can of fruit juice and weighs only ten pounds. It can be carried about easily and is most valuable in an emergency or at a place where there is no X ray available.

These are only some of the things that atoms can do for us. Atomic energy is still young. In the years to come, there will be many changes. During your lifetime, the peaceful atom should make the world an easier, healthier, happier place!

64

radioisotope machine

APPENDIX

Some other important atomic pioneers:

Chadwick, James: Discovered the neutron in 1932.

Joliot-Curie, Irene and Frederic: Daughter of Marie and Pierre Curie, and her husband. Were the first to make artificial radioisotopes in 1933.

Rutherford, Ernest: Worked out the nature of radioactivity in 1902, discovered the nucleus of the atom in 1911, and split the first atom in 1919.

Soddy, Frederic: Discovered isotopes in 1910.

Urey, Harold: Discovered hydrogen's heavy isotope, deuterium, in 1932.

GLOSSARY

AEC   Atomic Energy Commission (U.S.) All atomic energy in the United States is under the control of the AEC. The Commission is in charge of the sources, manufacture, and uses of all fissionable materials. It has important programs of research, building, training, and information.

artificial element   A chemical element that does not exist in nature but which can be made in an atomic reactor.

atomic furnace   An atomic reactor.

canal   A tank of water which is used to hold dangerously radioactive materials in order to protect workers.

coffin   A thick metal box which is used to hold very radioactive material.

contaminated	Anything that has accidently become radioactive.
cool off	To stop being radioactive. Some materials have to cool off before they can be handled safely.
critical size	The smallest amount of atomic fuel that will allow a chain reaction to take place.
curie	The unit used to measure radiation. It is equal to the amount of radiation given off by one gram of radium in one second.
Einstein, Albert	(1879-1955), born in Germany, fled under Hitler, and became an American citizen in 1940. In 1905 he published a brilliant theory which became the basis for the discovery of atomic energy. The theory stated that neither matter nor energy can ever be destroyed, but that matter can be changed into energy. Einstein expressed this in the equation $E = mc^2$. It means that energy (E) is equal to mass (m) multiplied by the speed of light (c), multiplied by itself. Mass is the amount of material or matter in anything. The speed of light is 186,000 miles a second.
emit	To give off. Radioactive substances emit rays.
enriched uranium	Ordinary uranium which has fissionable uranium added to it.

69

fissionable	Usable as an atomic fuel. A material whose atoms will split.
fusion	A source of atomic energy which is the opposite of fission. Instead of nuclei being split, they are forced together. The energy of the sun is released by fusion.
hot	Radioactive.
moderator	A material which is used in an atomic reactor to slow down the speed of the neutrons. Graphite and water are common moderators.
nuclear energy	The correct name for energy produced by changes in atomic nuclei. *Atomic energy* is the common name for nuclear energy.
pig	Heavy metal container for radioactive material. Similar to *coffin*.
pitchblende	The ore richest in uranium.
remote manipulator	A device that can handle radioactive materials mechanically while the operator remains safe behind a shield. (Also called a *master slave manipulator*.)
scram	To stop an atomic reactor. An emergency stop is called a *fast scram*.
transmute	To change one kind of atom into another kind.

INDEX

Roentgen, Wilhelm K., 18

Savannah, 48, 49

thorium, 23, 30
tracers, 53

uranium, 20, 29, 30, 32, 43
uranium-234, 29
uranium-235, 29, 46
uranium-238, 29, 46

X rays, 18, 64